A-way With Words...

Poetry Buy the Book

An Eclectic Collection
By
Carolyn Merrifield Christiel

Featuring
Kelly Elizabeth Christiel

iUniverse, Inc.
New York Lincoln Shanghai

A-way With Words...
Poetry Buy the Book

iUniverse, Inc.

For information address:
iUniverse, Inc.
2021 Pine Lake Road, Suite 100
Lincoln, NE 68512
www.iuniverse.com

ISBN: 0-595-30448-6

Printed in the United States of America

A-way With Words...

03/31/07

Dear Mary Alice,

May God bless
and keep you and make His face
to shine upon you and yours always —

Love,
Carolyn Christie

May our words inspire
and your heart enjoy
A-way With Words!
Kelly Christie

To God—Thank you for my life,
                    my loves,
                    my gifts,
                    and your grace.

To my Momma—This book is for you.
                    You were always my inspiration-always.
                    (And by the way, that umbilical cord cutting thing
                    just didn't work.)

To my Daddy—You were my first love
                    (You showed me what to look for in a man.)

To my Man—You are my rising sun,
                    My breath of fresh air…
                    My ever luminous moon.

Contents

Introduction . . . . *ix*

Author's Note . . . . *xi*

Segment 1—It's Only the Beginning 1
    Roots • I Wish That I Could See My Face • Mikie • My Melt Away Snowman • black widow • A Child's Prayer • October • While Traveling • I Know My Parents Love Me • School Is the Cool Place 2B • go go goldilocks

Segment 2—A Little Depressed...You Think? 13
    Way Back Last Week—When I Was Happy • Damn Monday • he loves me • i live in a galaxy of stars • confused • Looking Low • i am lost

Segment 3—Looking Up and Laughing 21
    Your Present • An Ode to Eddie • Upon the Birth of Your First Baby Girl • You're Not the Godmother, But You're All Right • Retiring Raliegh • Love Is Beautiful • My Future Retirement Speech

Segment 4—Definitely Deep 29
    The Love Machine • Friends • Sonnet #1 • My Love • Sonnet #2

Segment 5—Fundamentally Family .35
    Losing My Mama • "My Boys" • Revs. • Losing Papi • A Tribute to My Mother • My Brother, MY Friend. I Have Two Fathers in Heaven Now • My Daddy • Grandma • It's a Brother Thing • Forever Love • My Little Sister Le Le Leah • A Daughter Is A Gift for Life • Cathy's Getting Married • Baby Barker • My Dearest Friend • To All My Girls • Just So You Know • O • Leah's One, Chuckie's Two • My Angel

Segment 6—I Love My Sweetheart-Husband 60
    misunderstanding • My Haikuski Love • To C.J.C.—Wanting You • Love Poem • He Loves Me Anyway *To My Sweetheart • I Realize, I Do • Love

C-3 • How Do I Love Thee…Let Me Count the Ways • Love-N-You • The Love of My Life

Segment 7—The Kelly Creations 72

the sun shines in the sky like a • Rain, Wind, Snow, Sun, Hail • My Everything Was You • His Breath • His Breath   Part II • To My Daddy • As a child she was liked but not loved • a queen, lovely indeed • Womanly

About the Authors *83*

Introduction

This book was born to bring comfort, humor, understanding, empathy, sympathy, and plain old love to all whom hug it.

See yourself or someone you know reflected in each piece. Do not expect symmetry, as the world pretty much isn't symmetrical. Rather, expect to experience the ups and downs and ins and outs of life and love.

Please enjoy…and A-WAY WITH WORDS!

Author's Note

I love to write! Creative expression through poetry just comes naturally for me. It beats my heart to connect to others by way of "the written word." If I can make another person laugh, cry, or just say, "Write on!" I'm elated.

So read it, enjoy it, love it-I hope-and as with *all* love-share it!

God bless you.

C.C.

A special thank-you goes out to my brother-in-law, Lloyd K. Winston, for all of his hard work in the assembly and processing of this project. More thanks to all who offered and helped make this dream come true!

Segment 1
It's Only the Beginning

Roots

Roots—spreading continuously—
Gathering each part of us and dying

Come to life, oh roots,come to
Life again so that I may live—

Live and love and grow more roots—
And then, my people shall never die

1971

I Wish That I Could See My Face

I wish that I could see my face
Instead of that same old reflection

I want to see my eyes, my nose, and my mouth—
My ears, and oh yeah, my complexion

Oh heck, I can't even see my neck
And don't care to as much as my face

I can see yours and the lady's next door
But none of that's taking the place

If the fact that unless something "too cool" occurs
Causing me to see what *you* see—

What you and everyone else seems to know...
That I look exactly like me!

2001

Mikie

Mikie just sat there with nothing to say.
He sat and he sat and he sat all day.
When asked "What's the matter?"
as he turned from his pose
And smiled when he answered
"I'm asleep—only my eyes forgot to close!"

1971

My Melt Away Snowman

I had a little snowman
I made him yesterday
This morning when I went out to play
My melt away snowman
Was melting away

I made another snowman
I made him nice and fat
I went into the closet
To get my father's hat

The very next day
When I went out to play
My melt away snowman
Was melting away

1960

black widow

"black widow, black widow,
how many legs you got?"

"not enough to take care of my children and chores
since my husband was shot"

"black widow, black widow,
how did your husband die?"

"he died in a war which wasn't his own—
he died alone."

1971

A Child's Prayer

God in heaven, take care of me
(Though your face I cannot see)
Trust is what I have in you
Your miracles will see me through
God, your love has set me free
(I pray I'll make you proud of me!)

1991

October

October is the month for fun
The weather's changed, the summer's done

It's autumn and leaves are everywhere
We're back in school, the playground's bare

The wind is blowing, the sun's still bright
Though it's not March you could fly a kite

The footballs are spiraling, the pumpkins are back
And soon they'll turn into Lanterns O' Jack

Frost himself for sure will be here
October, October…the fun month of the year!

2000

While Traveling

While traveling I've seen sights
up high on flights
down low in cars
I've seen all types of flowers, plants,
and trees
Flown through all kinds of weather
and clouds over seas

But I think I've enjoyed most
My travels by foot

'Cause then I can walk, run, skip
Or stay put.

2000

I Know My Parents Love Me

I know my parents love me
They leave me hints—they do
They teach me well, keep me healthy and safe
And kinda understand me too

They know what makes me happy
Can't take it when I'm sad
Provide for me the things in life
It seems they never had

But most of all they show their love
They hug and kiss me too
They're with me when the day begins
And always when it's through

I'm grateful that I have them
I love them more each day
I know my parents love me
It shows in every way!

2001

School is the Cool Place 2B

School is the cool place 2B
If you want 2 learn 2 read and write
And all about history

If you want 2 do math C movies
Hear tapes do experiments N science galore

Piece puzzles 2 gether, solve problems,
Think hard go on trips and meet people 4 sure

Then take it from me—I've been going 4 years
And U can 4 yourself truly C

You'll be learning discerning and
Yearning 4 more...

Yes School is the cool place 2B!

2001

Go Go Goldilocks
You may not come again
Get yourself fast from this house
Before I count to ten

Go Go Goldilocks
You've done so very wrong
Broke in stole food defaced a chair
And took a nap—Begone!

Go Go Goldilocks
Your mom would have a fit
She'd not be very proud of you
Pulling this stupid...bit!

1990

Segment 2
A Little Depressed...You Think?

Way Back Last Week—
When I Was Happy

Seems so long ago
Things were normal—status quo
But now I weep
So out of control
Chaos confusion frenzied unhinged…
Seems so long ago
When I was happy

Damn Monday

Ugly.
All is ugly on Monday.
Yes, me and *you* too.
It's the beginning of something that
     probably wouldn't come to fruition anyway—
Death comes on Monday.
All evils within us use Monday
     as their scapegoat.
I've never hated before—
Hope to never again
But Monday—I hate you.

1972

He loves me.

He loves me not.

He loves me!

He loves me not.

He loves me!!

He loves me!!!

He loves me!!!!

He loves me not—

I knew it was too good to be true.

1972

i live in a galaxy of stars
yet i am but a speck in the sky
i mingle amongst a cast of thousands
though I am but an understudy

my plight is simple
i am without one
but what's so sad is that no one cares
at least I don't think so
and what's truly so bad is
neither do I

1972

Confused—I just don't know what
    the world expects of me—do you?
Turning down a one-way street
Yells and screams of "Will she make it?"
"Probably not—there's too much against her"
Herself, basically.
She undergoes the terrors and
    consequences of an unforseen world
She tries—but only in vain, for as
    it goes, she fails one more time.
As usual.

                                        1971

Looking Low

Depleted
>existing between a living hell
and death
>trapped behind earth's heavy
walls of hatred
>begging to be free
i am not obliged
i must endure this unbearable lifestyle

Me alone
>alone and undecided, unaware—
>>extremely cautious
>too cautious
>walking through space tripping
>>over nothing but unhappiness
>>and despair

Changes?
>yes changes ensue
>>changes from bad to an
>>inconceivable worse
>>negativeness prevails and
>>once again…
>>>I lose

1972

I am lost
People walk over around
And through me
Don't they see me?
Don't they care?
I've tried; I look about
my being in search of someone
to be
But I am always only
the me nobody sees

1972

Segment 3
Looking Up and Laughing

Your Present

Here be a check
It might look kinda good
But wait until tomorrow
For it to do what it should

1999

An Ode to Eddie

Con Man Eddie was his name
Messin' over women was his claim to fame
He lied to each one with the straightest face
And he always managed to keep them in place
See he was the "boss man" they'd do as he'd say
Eddie never realizing that one day he'd pay
                    one day he'd pay
                    one day he'd pay

He'd never foresee that—he knew he was cool
His professional line always worked on some fool
But times have changed and things are slow
And old Con Man Eddie has nowhere to go
                    nowhere to go
                    nowhere to go

The young girls use him now—he plays to their rap
Yes proverbial Eddie fell into his own trap

Upon the Birth of Your First Baby Girl

Sookie, I'm so happy for you, honey
God's blessed you with that Eloise, it's true
In just one wink of an eye, your personal life is over
And baby stuff is all you'll know to do.

We've been through 'bout a million things together
Ups downs ins outs over many years
We've shared a bunch of happy times together
As fate would have it, also shed some tears

So know that I will always be there for you
Our friendship is forever—it will keep
'Cept don't be calling me for a.m. feedings
'Cause, girlfriend, my black a__ is gon' be sleep

1981

You're Not the Godmother,
But You're All Right

You're not the godmother, but you're all right
Mess with "Carole's kids" and you'll get a fight
You care for each one with the greatest of ease
You capture their attention
Your heart they seize
And then your give them your love
   and you always please
You're not the godmother, but you're all right
You keep my baby, every Thursday night
And do a good job prob'ly 'cause she's so
   light-like-you
You're on call be it day or night…
You're not the godmother, but you're—
   Don't call you Phyllis or Lane
You're not the godmother, but you're allright!

Retiring Raliegh

Raliegh, let me tell you the new rules around this place
Now that you'll be habitually here
There are some tasks you must face

You'll be driving me to work and back
Running errands while I'm gone
Cleaning the house and cooking my meals
And taking good care of the lawn

You must pay the bills, answer the calls
Straighten the basement and sweep the halls
And then my dear when you are through
I'll come on home to take care of you!

1987

Love Is Beautiful

Love is beautiful, love is kind
Love is the punk that left me behind
Behind in a world that doesn't care
Love again? I couldn't dare

Love is beautiful, love is kind
Love is just something to kick your behind
Kick your behind in a world that don't care
Love again? I wouldn't dare

Love is beautiful, love is kind
Simply a punk that kicks your behind
And leaves you alone in a world that won't care
Love again? I couldn't
        I wouldn't
        I shouldn't
        I think I'll dare!

1972

My Future Retirement Speech

Working with you all was sometimes fun
Especially once the live long day was done
I did my best
Forgot the rest
Sincerely hope
I passed the test
10-4, good buddies
I bid adieu
Replacement team, it's now on you!

1980

Segment 4
Definitely Deep

The Love Machine

Twisting   Turning   Agitating
The Love Machine
He's here when you need him
Ready to please
He'll turn you on
The Love Machine

Steady   Sure   Precise
Your desires—his command
Exacting your senses
Encroaching upon your conception of
"What it is"

But don't be deceived
Tho he'll love you
Never leave you
Be the peak of perfection
He's only The Love Machine

1972

Friends

Friends—
   God's little leaves from the tree of love
Growing, living, laughing,
   crying together in a lifetime
Friends are there when needed—
   giving, feeling, caring for each other

Friend,
   Our love for you will never end
You're in our thoughts, our memories, our hearts
For in our lives you've played a big part
We'll miss you
God's leaf from the tree of love
We were put here together by our God above

Sonnet 1

I remember the day that I met you
Strong, determined, and hard as hell to please
I sensed that in time our love would grow true
If not, your love I would just have to seize

Time passed by quickly, not making a sound
Leaves and flowers died; no doubt they were tired
Just as I, waiting for your love I'd found
My dreams and hopes had in some way expired

Each day I lived without you seemed unfair
As a winter flower that has not died
Life had become even harder to bear
My thoughts of you—proving that I'd tried

With the spring flowers that blossomed and grew
Returned my old thoughts and new love for you

1972

My Love

My love
For you shall never cease
Our hearts are joined
Forever as one

You are with me always
As I breathe
As I think
As I love our children...
Extensions of us

My love
For you shall live on
God blessed our love
Forever as one

for Mildred

1999

Sonnet 2

Triumphantly she stood, her head held high
She knew her beauty, birthed by nature grew
Like night that pours out mystic darkness spills
The meaning and the sense of truths unknown

Her smile which lit the souls of those who saw
The love and life that shone so in her eyes
For she was life itself and well she knew
Her body had brought forth a world delight

Her baby son, as good and fine as she
Assured the world that sin would be removed
As life seems often gone at winter's birth
Her full grown son did die at our expense

And there she stood once more her head held high
The Black Madonna knew her son still lived

1972

Segment 5
Fundamentally Family

Losing My Mama

Losing my mama was an actual process
At first it just seemed kinda natural—
She was sick, seen to, and pretty much recovered—
But then came the *real* serious
Is she gonna die?" stuff
It was hard to take
And we took it over and over again…
But we prayed
And God took care of everything.

She was not really the same anymore
But she was similar to herself
And she and we dealt with
The obvious changes and challenges. I didn't think
I always did so well with it, but I tried.
I criticized, questioned, and cried,
But I tried.

Then, the last call—"Your Mom is sick—come now"
I came. She went. But before she left
God granted us time time to converse a bit—
Not really say goodbye, but to see her go
(something I never wanted to do)

We were rendered so helpless, so unhappy, so
Lost, yet I know that in time
God will heal my thoughts, my hurts, my sorrow
I know God is taking care of my mother's very soul

Losing my mama was not easy; God,
However, ordered every step.
We took those steps…
And then they disappeared.

2000

My Boys

Didn't birth them
Didn't have to—
Want some kids?
God'll send 'em to you.
Went to bed on a Saturday night without even one
By Sunday night, poof!—1-2-3 the job was done.
Had three boys now, house filled with boats, cars, trains, and kiddie
    stuff—
Didn't take too long to realize
I'd had just about enuff!!
But I loved my man and his kids were he
And I knew I'd adjust—that's the way it would be
So in no time flat love prevailed, life was them
Still drove me mad, but I recognized 3 gems.
As time passed by they grew—
And more and more I knew
        They were mine
The boys kept us busy—we gave and we took
We tried to raise them by the book
Sometimes we passed—sometimes we flawed
We never gave up though—we remained in awe.
All grown up now and on their own
I'd not be the same if their love I'd not known.
Hope in return my love for them shone…
God, I thank you for
        My Boys

2003

Revs.

As Revs go and come and go—
I'm glad you came.
Since meeting, knowing, and being your friend
I just ain't been the same.
You have been and continue to be
A part of us—of mine—of me
And so—just to let you know…
Rev, I appreciate and love you so
Stay in my life
Pray God's speed that we strive
And I will pray for you and yours—
Just always keep the doors
Of the church and your heart
Open forever!

God bless you!

for Wanda Y.

2003

Losing Papi

Check it out—I get a call from
my dad saying, "I'll be there soon.
I've packed my bags, sold the farm
And I'm coming to live with you!"

Tensions arise—"What am I going
To do with this old man? I have a
Lifestyle, you know; patterns, sequences,
And such. Where does he fit in?"
I ponder, he comes, we adjust.

At first it's not so bad, as he is relatively
Self-sufficient. Time passes—health falters.
"Eat, Papi—take your medicine, Papi.
"You're *not* the boss of me, Papi."

I see the sun fading in his very eyes
The earth won't shake 'cause he just
Doesn't dance as much as he used to
The moon—oh, the moon is coming up.

We attend the funeral of my uncle
His brother and I watch closely as
My dad weakens. Thoughts crowd my
Head—could he be next? No, of
Course not! It just won't happen!

It's dark now. The sun has yet to show
Its face and my Papi—my Papi
Has ridden away with the moon.

for Leila

2001

A Tribute to my Mother

Mothering is not as easy chore;
Perseverance, kindness, and work is in store
The words below attempt to detail
"Your Mothering"—the points that make you prevail.

M   is for Memories of my happy childhood
O   is for Offering me the best of you
T   is for Tolerance year after year
H   is for your Helping Hand; however, whenever, whatever
E   is for Every Exceptional quality you possess
R   is for Respect—both taught and displayed
I   is for Inheritance (I hope I'm like you!)
N   is for Never-ending love and concern
G   is for Granting (with God's help) the gift of life for me

Mama, with all my heart and soul
I want you to know this day
That I thank, appreciate, and love you
Much more than these words could ever convey
It is my prayer that over the years
I have made you proud in return
And have grown in the proper direction
Through all of the love you have shown

My Brother, My Friend

Robert, I miss you already, it's true
but I'm blessed with my many
sweet memories of you—
Your "baby" days when you'd let
ME "dry-your-tears"

Our growing up together sharing
good times, praying out fears

Your positive approach to life-
so easy, so mellow—
so hard working, self reliant,
determined and a "DAPPER"
kind-of-fellow

Your family always came first
no matter the time or the weather
You always set "the right example"
such a teacher—SO TOGETHER!

God did a magnificent job of
molding you, BLUE-
He planted the seed and from
it you grew…

You sprinkled your love over
everyone you knew-
MY BROTHER, MY FRIEND
I LOVE YOU

For Mary

1997

I Have Two Fathers in Heaven Now

I have two fathers in heaven now
I am blessed to have each one
One affords me loving memories—
One keeps me from coming undone

They both gave me life (I'm quite happy to say)
They both taught me well
How to fight, how to pray

I call one "Daddy," oh so loving and giving
So strong, so courageous—
Worked real hard for a living

I call the other "Father, "always with me no matter
Shields and protects me
Won't allow me to shatter

I need them both so much as they both made me *me*
They've helped me to grow on a positive path
Fair and faithful they've taught me to be

Without the direction of both my fathers above
I'd not have received so much
Nor known just how to love

Daddy, I thank you with all my heart
For the wonderful times we've had
I will always be your little girl
You will forever by my Dad

And God above, I thank you
For everything you do

You gave me the world's greatest daddy—
Now he's safe back at home with you.

for Valerie

1999

My Daddy

It was love at first touch, smell, sight
My daddy was wonderful, did everything right—
In my eyes

Daddy, I miss your presence while
your sprit lives on within me.
I find myself reflecting many
"Charles-isms"—even when they're not politically correct.
I'm ever so proud of them 'cause I remember
I'm you

Daddy, you kept me so happy and so secure for inasmuch as
I yearn to touch you, to see you, to hug you tight
My memories of you keep me satisfied…for now

2001

Grandma

Full of family pride with a
deep-seated faith in God
humble and modest manner
eager and anxious to help
always with the unmatched ability
to turn all frowns into smiles
         tears into joy and
         fears into fried chicken

1990

It's a Brother Thing...

It's a brother thing, you wouldn't understand.
Protecting you
Advising you
Bossing you around and telling on you

It's a brother thing, you couldn't understand.
Taking you for granted as you do the same
Calling each other something other than each other's name
Private sibling jokes abound without a bit of shame

It's a brother thing, you might not understand.
Obtrusion
Illusion
Underlying love the conclusion

It's a brother thing...
Maybe you understand.

God bless your soul, Chuckie

1997

Forever Love

I love you for all the reasons
Through every season
I'd commit treason to be by your side

I love your waking smile
I love your style
Please stay awhile—with me

2001

My Little Sister Le Le Leah

We never *really* knew from whence she came
I've teased her throughout the years
Assuring her that we did in fact "find her at the dump"
I just remember our parents dressing her (and us) in stripes—every
    picture sporting horizontal lines "taking over"

I remember our dad picking her up from the hospital and bringing
    her home in that yellow blanket
They said she was a girl (you see, she had no hair!) so I believed them
    and
defended her when the kids referred to her
as my little brother.

Years passed. The usual little sister problems arose and fell
    (I think I was kind of a mean big sister—oops—so, so sorry)
All those years of our parents saying "You'd better learn to be nice to
    each other; one day you'll be all each other has."

Well, we are now at that point in life
I didn't know back then that a sister is really truly your best friend—
Formed from the same clay, knowing you better than you know
    yourself and
loving you anyway

I had to finally realize that the person you didn't want to be bothered
    with is now the person you can't wait to see, to share with, to love,
    to talk to, to laugh at and with, and to play with—
Yes, *now* you want to play with her.

My little sister, Le Le Leah. She's so real, so tough, so cool—Never
    anybody's fool
She's intelligent, aware and comforting

Accomodating to a fault (Nana, Auntie & Momma blood running
    through her)
She's well taught.

I'd never ever trade her
She's one of a kind
I've been blessed by God above with her
My little sister's mine.
I love you, Leah

2003

A Daughter is a Gift for Life

When you're given a daughter
so precious, so sweet
You pray that her needs
You'll be able to meet

You dress her like the dolls
You once had long ago
You teach her and take her
Wherever you go

You try to protect her
From hurt, harm and shame
You try to hold on—
To keep her's your aim

But sooner or later
You see she has grown
She's anxious, determined
To be on her own

But wait, just wait…
If you loved her real good
Let her go and she'll come back for you
Like you knew she would

2001

Cathy's Getting Married

Cathy Martin is her name
If she gets on Ronnie's nerves
It'll surely stay the same
She wears that makeup
And dresses real cool
She's even gotten smarter,
She's nobody's fool—nobody's fool
Cathy finally finished college
At the age of 93
Hoping that one day
A teacher she'd be
Well she is one now,
Teaching science, math, and gym
The girl is getting ready
To take care of him—to take care of him
And Archie her father
Is real happy now
At 95 she's leaving home
He doesn't care how
And Vivion her mother
Cries her eyes out each day
'Cause her little baby
Is going away—going away
We all wish her happiness
Blessings and joy
And that six months from now
It's a healthy baby boy

Baby Barker

From 8 to 80 (which is just around the bend)
You have and always will be my very best friend
Didn't like you much at first—so prissy, so smart
Didn't realize back then how much you'd play a big part in my life

Through the birthdays and deaths, the happys and sads
The graduations, sicknesses, celebrations we've had
We've been there for each other—no ifs ands or buts
We've shared each other's families, we've spilled our very guts

You are my personal very best friend
Sent by God to me way long ago
My family is your family
We all just love you so

2001

My Dearest Friend

My dearest friend, what on earth would I do
If I had to go through this life without you?
You never neglect me, you're always right there
I depend on your friendship, your kindness, your care.
You're the eternal problem solver, a helper just and fair
So very loyal and patient, your first name should be "Share."
I will go on forever appreciating you
May God eternally bless your heart—for doing what you do.

2001

To All My Girls

To all my girls
(And you know who you are)
I love each and every one of you
As you have taken me farther than
I thought I'd ever fly—
Thanks to you I've succeeded
I've reached for the sky
I've even touched a star or two
Your confidence in and love for me
Has gotten me through, has set me free!

2001

Just So You Know
A poem for my husband and for my dearest friend

...You've got all the answers
and you love to share—
even when nobody asked you
AND DON'T NOBODY CARE!

2001

O.
(a.k.a. L.G....B.B.)

Hey little girl,
Got some stuff for you to do
Pick me up—take me there
And bring me home too!
And on the way will you please let me pay
A bill or two or three?
And on the way back let's drive through for a snack
(You're way too good to me!)
yes, you're on my list of slavelets—
I let you do things for me
And if you play your cards just right
You can keep on being my friend, O.B.

2002

Leah's One, Chuckie's Two

Leah's one's my godchild/niece
Though Chuckie's two came first
I love the three of them so hard
Sometimes I think I'll burst
From the love and emotions all bottled inside
(Guess now I'm a crying old aunt)
I love these three 'kateers more than life itself
(They say they love me too though I don't deign flaunt)
there's Rachie and Reesie and Zanne, oh my
I remember each coming to be
To heck with their parents (my siblings)
I felt God had just sent them to me!
I cared for each one, changed those diapers and fed
Took them on trips, got them ready for bed
All I ever wanted or needed in return is that
They call me "Auntie"—and that my love they'd learn.

2003

My Angel

Of all the babies in the world
Ever thought of, conceived, and birthed—
you were the best baby

of all the children on God's green earth—
you were the most delightful

Count every teen
Far, near, and in between—
you were fantastic!

You are now the most amazing young adult I know
I've loved every phase of your existence
You are my blessing...
My very evidence of love!

2003

Segment 6
I Love My Sweetheart-Husband
(Had You Heard?)

Misunderstanding
Not enough time
All seem to enter into our private lifestyles
Personal feelings go unexpressed
Many inner conflicts anxieties hopes—depressed

Being unsure of what to expect—of what is expected
Afraid to delve deeper—just might be rejected

Wanting needing begging pleading with myself
As well as
        Wanting you to want
        Needing you to need
        Begging you to plead

Your position, so confident, exact
Mine so unsettled, insecure, yielding
So fearful that I might emerge into happiness
But all the while still not quite certain
Why this self denial should bring such hurtin' inside me

Mostly self inflicted
Always stand convicted of the trials and
Tribulations that I bring upon myself

But don't try to change me
Never rearrange me for to be the me I want to be
I must do it on my own

Don't rush me, don't wait
We could leave it to fate but—
It just might be too late—and besides
When I have found myself
It is only then that I can offer me to you

1972

My Haikuski Love

Whenever I see
The man with whom I'm in love
My heart skips a beat

1999

To C.J.C.—Wanting You

Leaving me   Wanting you
Your smile, your tender touch
Vaguely a picture in my mind
Worn to bits and pieces by its constant usage

What was once you
Has been pre-empted by a dream
A dream molded firmly in my brain
Oh, I don't like this vicarious living
Dying inside with desire

All the many plans—harshly blown away
Like the winter wind
By your absence

I should go on, venture into another's life
But how can I when
You've become so much a part of me
And how can I when
I've left my strength, my heart, my love
With you?
You've left me   Still wanting you.

1973

Love Poem

My arms are ever open
To hold you close to my heart
Is ever wishing for your love
To mix wth the love within
My mind and soul and body
That lives for you

1972

He Loves Me Anyway

I'm so blessed 'cause my
man loves me anyway

When I'm good or bad
happy or sad
Up down and all around

Yes, he questions fusses and
pleads and we
Just don't ALWAYS agree—
But after at least two
sunsets, maybe three

He let's it go
And don't you know
Through it all
Come winter through fall
Er day—Mr. Magnificent Man
Just loves me ANYWAY!

2003

To My Sweetheart

My love for you is everlasting
Our souls are intertwined
We've made the "love connection"
We are conjoined at the heart

I Realize, I Do

I realize, I do
It's all because of you
That I live happily with joy
From the love of the boy
God sent to me

I realize, I do
That even moments without you
Are mere fragments of time
With no reason, no rhyme
Blank space
With no place to be

I realize, I do
Pure goodness with you
Your endless loyalty
Your being happy with me
Makes me clearly see
My blessings

I realize, I do
How much I love you

2002

Love C-3

C_1

Love and you seem so near
Yet at a distance still
Like the sky at the ocean's end
Something to hope for

C_2

Because I am involved in your world of uncertainty
I am pretty much unsure myself
Discovery and rediscovery keep me going—
What makes you tick?
I know these times find you searching. Seeking
Trying to grasp you and yours—
Just keep in mind that you can always find
Me and mine right here…
And we can wait

C_3

The thought of you upsets my soul
Like the sound of thunder on a sunny day—
You surprise me, invite me to wonder
When I think of you I envisage your face
As brown and handsome as autumn
I hear your voice, reeking with masculinity
I long to touch you, to hold you, to know you
You possess the warmth and tenderness I need
You

How Do I Love Thee?...Let Me Count the Ways

There aren't enough numerals designed on earth
To count all the ways my husband is worth
The love he is given by God and by me
For being the wonderful man with the key to my heart

I love him for his selflessness
He always puts God first
I love him for his humility, honesty, and humor
(He's so funny I could burst)
I love him for his loyalty and charitable ways
He's generous to a fault
(Despite his meager early days)
He's a super father, a hard worker, and good friend
He also kisses real, real good upon each blessed day's end

I'm so grateful God gave me this man to love and share my life...
I love him every way love is—I'm proud to be his wife.

PS. And he's cute, too!

2002

Love-N-You

For all the things you've said and done
For all the ways my heart you've won
For all the trials as well as fun...
I thank you

The way you melt my heart—oh my!
How everything is you and I
Without you I would surely die...
I need you

Your walk, your voice, your magic touch
Your smile, your hug, your kiss and such
All add to just how very much
I want you

Yes, you were made by God above
Who sent me you and all your love
Like black on tar like hand in glove
I love you

1994

The Love of my Life

When I was a young child, I knew I'd meet the man of my dreams
one day.

I knew he would be you.

That business about "Prince Charming" & "tall, dark, and
handsome"—Though you fit the bill perfectly, you are more the
epitome of "smart, soulful, charismatic, and kind."

That is what we girls should be looking for.

That's what I'm talking about.

As the love of my life you've been met with challenges, obstacles, and
bunches of crap—sorry for some of that!

I'm praying the love you share with me supersedes all the problems
we see.

You are the man I was waiting for.

You came to me proper and right.

You are my tangible "dream come true"

I had faith and God brought you to light.

Amen!

2003

Segment 7
The Kelly Creations

The sun shines in the sky like a
Glittering armor just passing by
With a knight and a tall horse—
What a beautiful sight!
The knight and the horse—
Just looking at me
I stopped and I thought
"What does he do on the battlefield?
Does he dream, does he fight,
Or is he just a king with a shining light?"

1990

Rain, Wind, Snow, Sun, Hail

Sometimes the rain brings memories. It always gets me thinking of
past loves.
The wind rushes by and takes pain away from my heart.

The snow covers and shields me from empty promises. The sun melts
the snow and makes puddles from the tears I've cried. The hail
beats like a drum on my mind, reminding me that you went away.

1993

My Everything Was You

Even in a room seating hundreds of people
I saw row G seat 2 and only noticed you
And from that moment
I knew my everything would be you

Years flew and our love grew and my love for you
Something that you couldn't deny
Making your problems mine
and your heartache mine too
Leaving you is something I'll never dream to do

You were my every reason for living
Too much of me is what I was giving
I spent way too many nights crying
Knowing that my love for you was dying

Unable to smile all the while
keeping the pain inside
Even though it was so hard to hide
My everything was you and this is something you knew

You lied
I cried
You cheated
I pleaded

It's over now but even in a room
filled with hundreds of people
If you were in row G seat 2
I would still notice you

His Breath

His breath…stinking like a pot of day ol' cabbage
Approached me like a gamesman to a deer
Where you been? When did you get here?
Why didn't you call?
His words shoot at me like a rifle
I smile, making my answers quick and
straight to the point
On vacation, yesterday, and
because I lost your number is what I say
When I'm really thinking: I was hiding from you
I wish I was still there so I wouldn't have to talk to you
And I tossed your number in the garbage
the same day you gave it to me
But that would be rude
And if I said those things he would probably think
I was as arrogant as a Siamese cat.
Sweating like a hooker in church, I tried to
Think of a way I could escape
The clutches of his conversation
We've talked about the weather,
the fight at the game, and everything
else under the sun.
When will it end!?!?! I scream out
in my head.
(Our conversation is as dull as pre-school
scissors and finally I can take no more.)
so I gave him gum like you would give
a quarter to a bum.
Walked away saying "Have a nice day."

2001

His Breath Part II

His breath…warm like sun rays
Shining down on my back,
Reminds me of the cool calm comfort
Of Chicago's lakefront on a summer night.

From his breath I can feel his soul
It's not like fire but,
Cool like mist and
Subtle like a rainbow after a storm

I can feel his breath on my shoulders
neck and ears
I can feel his breath when his
Mouth is nowhere near
His breath sends me to another world,
To tropic islands far away
On boat rides in the ocean and balloon rides
In the air.

His breath relieves my mind
Untwists knots in my body
And calms my nerves at day's end
Forget drugs cuz I've got his breath
Prozac and Ritalin are all things of the past
For it's the energy and comfort from his breath
That will make me last.

And this is just his breath.

To My Daddy

I never tell you as much as I should how much I love you.
I've got a lot of titles to uphold—like being a hard worker
                                    a good listener
                                    talented and sweet
But being daddy's little girl will always be most important in my heart.
You've always been there for me and I've been so blessed.
It's because of you I'm able to spot a real black man millions of miles away.
It's because of you that I know right from wrong.
                          good from bad, and
                          Gucci from Guess.
It is because of you that I am as bold as I am.

It is because of you that I know the difference between being black in America
                                    and being black period.
From you, Daddy, I received street smarts,
                          style, and
                          the courage to dare to be different.
Dad, you always wanted me to have what you didn't,
And even though you speak with a tight jaw and a stern look,
I want you to know that you are appreciated and loved by me always.
Thank you.

As a child she was liked but not loved

I mean, as a baby she never received too many kisses and a whole bunch of hugs.

Only received harsh words from a mother who rejected her past.

And through her seed the pain continued to fester and last.

Mommy on crack—Daddy straight whack—of course he wasn't around—and nestled in a ghetto in a structure that was unsettled—a difficult life Baby was bound.

Grandmommy didn't have enough shelter to even shield Baby's eyes and ears

Only person to ever even see Baby's painful tears.

Baby grows to teen unorganized in her thoughts

Not her fault—remember this is how Baby now teen was taught

More concerned with her looks instead of books

Fascinated by things that go bling

Not worried about education and success but obsessed with material things.

Virgin until the age of thirteen

Not knowing the pain that sex without love brings.

Walked the cold, hard streets of Chicago, Illinois

Playing too many games, acting like life was a toy

Her philosophy: college—why bother?

Husband? I'd rather have a "baby father."

Crazy how time flies

Smoking all her problems away

Constantly staying high.

Not knowing that change could come to all who keep growing—

Just seventeen and at four months she's already showing.

Dealt with the wines, drug dealers, and street life.

Wanting more, like one day being somebody's sweet wife.

Knowing a reactive cycle could kill her soul

So finding a higher power would be the only thing that could mend and keep her whole.

Thanks to the Creator up above
Twenty-three year old Mrs. Candice Jones and baby have more than
enough love.

2002

A queen, lovely indeed;
Mother, sister, cousin, but Aunty to me.
So much spirit
God gave Aunty life and she definitely lived it.

Now she's free, planted her seeds and watched them grow
Acknowledge her spirit, embrace he soul
Her beliefs were strong, her heart was too
We can use her past as a path
By realizing what Shiphrah went through.
Say what you want, feel what you like,
But the truth is Aunty Shiphrah
took a stand for all of our people and put up a good fight.

She always told me I could be a model
Maybe she meant runway or perhaps
A strong, black, positive model for all to see.
Whatever it was it's possible
Because of her blood that runs through me.

A queen, lovely indeed;
Mother, sister, cousin, but Aunty to me.
Aunty, you will be missed because you were loved.

2003

Womanly

She, Her, We, Me born with grace we are womanly
Sister, Daughter, Mother taught her just what a woman's supposed
to be.
Our spirit remains strong similar to Grandma or Nana who's gone.

She educated us not to put up a big fuss when man has done wrong.
"Just stay strong and keep on keeping on."
Cousin, Friend sharing tales that only women understand.
The vertebrae, the "everything's gonna be okay," the goddess of the
land.
As priceless as time
Unique and divine, we survive oppression, separation, childbirth, *and*
discrimination.
We are the nation.
We are the roots.
We are the buds.
We are the flowers in bloom that symbolize love.
We are womanly.

About the Authors

Carolyn Merrifield Christiel is a wife, mother, teacher, writer, certified lay speaker, and last but not least, a child of God. She finds a way to include poetry in practically everything she attempts. Carolyn has won numerous prizes, awards, and accolades for her writing and recitations throughout her life. Although poetry is her specialty, she expects to publish a book about her sons and daughter and several children's books in the future. She wants you to pray for her.

Kelly Elizabeth Christiel, delightful daughter, sister, and faithful friend, is a graduate of Lincoln University, holding a BS degree in journalism. Kelly is a natural, profound writer/poet. Keep your eyes and ears open for her-she's on her way. God bless her heart.

0-595-30448-6

Printed in the United States
72185LV00004B/304-321

9 780595 304486